THE RITE

OF THE

PASSION

ↀ

A PLAY BY
CHARLES WILLIAMS

ↀ

British Library Cataloguing-in-Publication Data
A catalogue record for this book is available from
the British Library

A HISTORY OF THE THEATRE

'The Theatre' is a collaborative form of fine art that uses live performers to present the experience of a real or imagined event. The performers may communicate this experience to the audience through combinations of gesture, speech, song, music, and dance, with elements of art, stagecraft and set design used to enhance the physicality, presence and immediacy of the experience. The specific place of the performance is also named by the word 'theatre' – derived from the Ancient Greek word *théatron*, meaning 'a place for viewing', itself from *theáomai*, meaning 'to see', 'watch' or 'observe'.

Modern Western theatre largely derives from ancient Greek drama, from which it borrows technical terminology, classification into genres, and many of its themes, stock characters, and plot elements. The city-state of Athens is where 'theatre' as we know it originated, as part of a broader culture of theatricality and performance in classical Greece that included festivals, religious rituals, politics, law, athletics, music, poetry, weddings, funerals, and symposia. Participation in the city-state's many festivals – and attendance at the City Dionysia as an audience member (or even as a participant in the theatrical productions) in particular, was an important part of citizenship.

The theatre of ancient Greece consisted of three types of drama: tragedy, comedy, and the satyr play (a form of tragicomedy, similar in spirit to the bawdy satire of burlesque). The origins of theatre in ancient Greece, according to Aristotle (384–322 BCE), the first theoretician of theatre, are to be found in the festivals that honoured Dionysus. These performances (the aforementioned City Dionysia) were held in semi-circular auditoria cut into hillsides, capable of seating 10,000–20,000 people. The stage consisted of a dancing floor (orchestra), dressing room and scene-building area (skene). Since the words were the most important part, good acoustics and clear delivery were paramount. The actors (always men) wore masks appropriate to the characters they represented, and each might play several parts.

Athenian tragedy (the oldest surviving form of tragedy) emerged sometime during the sixth century BCE, and flowered during the fifth century BCE – from the end of which it began to spread throughout the Greek world – and continued in popularity until the beginning of the Hellenistic period. Aeschylus, Sophocles, and Euripides were masters of the genre. The other side of the coin – Athenian comedy, is conventionally divided into three periods; 'Old Comedy', 'Middle Comedy', and 'New Comedy'. Old Comedy survives today largely in the form of the eleven surviving plays of Aristophanes, while Middle Comedy is largely lost (preserved only in a few relatively short fragments in authors such as Athenaeus of Naucratis). New Comedy is known primarily from the substantial papyrus fragments of Menander.

Western theatre developed and expanded considerably under the Romans. The theatre of ancient Rome was a thriving and diverse art form, ranging from festival performances of street theatre, nude dancing, and acrobatics, to the staging of Plautus's broadly appealing situation comedies, to the high-style, verbally elaborate tragedies of Seneca. Although Rome had a native tradition of performance, the Hellenization of Roman culture in the third century BCE had a profound and energizing effect on Roman theatre and encouraged the development of Latin literature of the highest quality for the stage. This tradition fed into the modern theatre we know today, and during the renaissance, theatre generally moved away from the poetic drama of the Greeks, and towards a more naturalistic prose style of dialogue. By the nineteenth century and the Industrial Revolution, this trend continued to progress.

In England, theatre was immensely popular, but took a big pause during 1642 and 1660 because of Cromwell's Interregnum. Prior to this, 'English renaissance theatre' was witnessed, with celebrated playwrights such as William Shakespeare, Christopher Marlowe and Ben Jonson. Under Queen Elizabeth, drama was a unified expression as far as social class was concerned, and the Court watched the same plays the commoners saw in the public playhouses. With the development of the private theatres, drama became more oriented towards the tastes and values of an upper-class audience however. By the later part of the reign of Charles I, few new plays were being written for the public theatres, which sustained themselves on the accumulated works of the previous decades. Theatre was now seen as something sinful and the Puritans tried very hard to drive it out of their society. Due to this stagnant period, once Charles II came back to the throne in 1660, theatre (among other arts) exploded with influences from France, and the wider continent.

The eighteenth century saw the widespread introduction of women to the stage – a development previously unthinkable. These women were looked at as celebrities (also a newer concept, thanks to ideas on individualism that were beginning to be born in Renaissance Humanism) but on the other hand, it was still very new and revolutionary. Comedies were full of the young and very much in vogue, with the storyline following their love lives: commonly a young roguish hero professing his love to the chaste and free minded heroine near the end of the play, much like Sheridan's *The School for Scandal*. Many of the comedies were fashioned after the French tradition, mainly Molière (the great comedic playwright), again harking back to the French influence of the King and his court after their exile.

After this point, there was an explosion of theatrical styles. Throughout the nineteenth century, the popular theatrical forms of Romanticism, melodrama, Victorian burlesque and the well-made plays of Scribe and Sardou gave way to the problem plays of Naturalism and Realism; the farces of Feydeau; Wagner's operatic *Gesamtkunstwerk*; musical theatre (including Gilbert and Sullivan's operas); F. C. Burnand's, W. S. Gilbert's and Wilde's drawing-room comedies; Symbolism; proto-Expressionism in the late works of August Strindberg and Henrik Ibsen; and Edwardian musical comedy. The list continues! These trends continued through the twentieth century in the realism of Stanislavski and Lee Strasberg, the political theatre of Erwin Piscator and Bertolt Brecht, the so-called Theatre of the Absurd of Samuel Beckett and Eugène Ionesco, and the rise of American and British musicals.

Theatre itself has an incredibly long history, and despite the massive proliferation of theatrical styles and mediums – it essentially owes its existence to the ancient Greeks and the Romans. The three main genres; tragedy, comedy and satyre, continue to influence plot themes, directing, writing and acting, with frequent and fascinating interrelations and overlaps. As a genre, it remains as popular today as it has ever been, and continues as a massive influence on popular culture more broadly. It is hoped that the current reader enjoys this book on the subject.

CHARLES WILLIAMS

Charles Walter Stansby Williams was born in London in 1886. He dropped out of University College London in 1904, and was hired by Oxford University Press as a proof-reader, quickly rising to the position of editor. While there, arguably his greatest editorial achievement was the publication of the first major English-language edition of the works of the Danish philosopher Søren Kierkegaard.

Williams began writing in the twenties and went on to publish seven novels. Of these, the best-known are probably *War in Heaven* (1930), *Descent into Hell* (1937), and *All Hallows' Eve* (1945) – all fantasies set in the contemporary world. He also published a vast body of well-received scholarship, including a study of Dante entitled *The Figure of Beatrice* (1944) which remains a standard reference text for academics today, and a highly unconventional history of the church, *Descent of the Dove* (1939). Williams garnered a number of well-known admirers, including T. S. Eliot, W. H. Auden and C. S. Lewis. Towards the end of his life, he gave lectures at Oxford University on John Milton, and received an honorary MA degree. Williams died almost exactly at the close of World War II, aged 58.

THE RITE OF THE PASSION

TALIESSIN'S SONG OF THE KING'S CROWNING

I SAW in the new-built city
   the King rise crowned;
his marches were ended,
   his heritage found.
With magians before him,
   bishops about,
poets sang to him,
   peasants cried out.
Logres lay round him,
   city-entwined,
the King in his kingdom,
   man in his mind.

I asked in a field of peasants
   Whence comes the King?
Short time from sowing
   spared they to sing.
One looked up, saying:
   All in our dearth
Arthur came to us
   as corn from earth.
He that plucks good wheat
   knows not how it grew,
so came King Arthur
   our famine through.

I asked in a hall of bishops
   Whence comes he?
Silent they gazed at
   Wise Canterbury:
Lo now, where Isaac's son
   (said he) *once slept*

TALIESSIN'S SONG OF THE KING'S CROWNING

down a great stairway
Arthur hath stept.
In vision I saw him
set foot on our ground,
even crowned as the least soul
God made is crowned.

I asked in a garden of poets
Whence comes the King?
Legend and fable
leapt they to sing.
Ah son of Brutus!
ah child of Troy!
Look how antiquity
breaks in new joy!
Yet one from southward
led all the choir,
singing a child that came
in a sea of fire.

I asked in a chamber of wizards
Whence comes he?
Sooth was their answer
or glamoury?
Marvellous ancestors
in a deep glass
through an aeon of aeons
caused they to pass:
fish and amphibia,
serpent and ape—
Human heart, human thought,
and human shape.

TALIESSIN'S SONG OF THE KING'S CROWNING

I asked in a hall of heralds:
What coat hath he borne?
They showed it: lo, azure,
    a unicorn
courant proper—ah so
    through a jungle he came!—
maned and unguled or,
    and gorged of the same
royally; a dragon
    couchant gules for crest;
the motto: Et homo rex
    factus est.

After some opening ceremony,[1] *the persons of the presentation enter in procession—a* HERALD *first, followed by five* MINSTRELS; *then, side by side,* JAMES *and* PILATE, PETER *and* CAIAPHAS, JOHN *and* HEROD, MARY *and* JUDAS; *after them, between* GABRIEL *and* SATAN, LOVE *vestmented in a crimson cope or other convenient apparel. The* MINSTRELS *take their places below the platform; the* HERALD *upon it at the front corner. The other persons are distributed about it,* LOVE'S *friends to his right, and his enemies to his left, he himself being at the back, with* GABRIEL *and* SATAN *on either hand. Each moves forward as he first speaks; thereafter they dispose themselves as may be agreed.*

[1] The hymns sung are given on p. 191.

PART I

Ho all you people, who are come
out of your huts through Christendom
in vigil here to bear a part,
being obedient to that art
whereby a new thing shall be made
and presently in you displayed
when nothing is that is not He,
enter into this mystery.

Ye who already out of dearth
find Him renewed within your earth,
who practised everywhere and long
submission to that only Strong,
growing more sure thereof by all
good or ill chance that did befall—
your end is found, your heart is He,
enter into this mystery.

Ye who go seeking Him and find
at whiles His breath within your mind,
but more of sighs and bloody tears,
nor any rescue through the years,
think that ye, being thus sacrificed,
image and are the death of Christ;
Despair ye? your despair is He;
enter into this mystery.

Ye to whom all His world is dark
save where He glows, a ruddy spark,
a natural portent, sent to show
who will not know Him still shall know;

6

He, thrust from peace, determines war,
and being not friend is conqueror—
yea, fear; yea, fly; exile is He—
enter into this mystery.

Behold, O people, as may fit
your reach and spiritual wit,
the tale of Golgotha the mount—
either that which gospellers recount,
or that which ye have found within
when in yourselves He is made sin:
Lift up your hearts: all this is He:
enter into this mystery.

Hear now the lords of heaven and hell—
God's swiftest runner, Gabriel,
the nuncio to the maid; and that
Satan, whom all ye marvel at:
not knowing him through your innermost,
dark viceroy of the Holy Ghost:
Lift up your hearts; these both are He—
enter into this mystery.

GABRIEL

I, Gabriel, stand up between earth and heaven;
　I am the troth in all hours tender and gay,
the giving of all things when all things are given;
　I am the right-hand pillar of the way.

SATAN

I, Satan, stand up between earth and heaven,
　I am contradiction and entire dismay;
the sharp divorce when all things are not given;
　I am the left-hand pillar of the way.

GABRIEL

I am the moment of presence and of vision,
  the undivined beheld, the unseen displayed,
o'ermounting the after anguish and derision;
  I am the salutation to the maid.

SATAN

I am the exile following in sorrow
  making man of that moment still afraid;
I am the mockery of the long to-morrow;
  I am the seven swords piercing thro' the maid.

GABRIEL

I am the light that comes in speed and wonder,
  the light that shines though the dark is not done,
dissolving the thick chains of hell asunder;
  I am the first gleam of the arisen Sun.

SATAN

I am the thick maze and the fond inventions
  whereby men hurry from repose to war,
I am the all but infinite dissensions,
  I am chaos and the love man hath therefor.

LOVE

But I am still the end and reconciling;
  I am all things driven on through hell to heaven;
I am the purifying and defiling,
  I am the union, perfected or riven.

There is none on earth that can have place beside me,
  nor any of all the angels that is God;
there is none can know what mysteries betide me
  who am those mysteries and their period.

Long since my first Nativity have ye studied
  when the Unsleeping Word at length found sleep,
and, after, went with head and side unbloodied,
  sowing the love that all his folk shall reap.

Remember the sweetness of that first salvation;
  yea, ere ye now to paths of Golgotha move,
renew, O people, the first adoration
  when your hearts fainted at the birth of Love.

One of the MINSTRELS

Three kings rode in to Bethlehem
  from Zion hastily:
when Joseph opened door to them
  they entered in all three.

The Child upon Our Lady's lap
  the kings bowed down before:
to see this wonder, by good hap,
  the slaves thronged at the door.

The first king fell upon his face:
  'O Child, a sign behold;
the princes of the Gentile race
  offer a gift of gold.'
Our Lady shuddered in her place:
  for riches men are sold.

'I wot that when thou goest up
  unto thy throne of might,
'tis I shall bear the golden cup,
  and come into thy sight.'

THE RITE OF THE PASSION
Humbly the second king kneeled down.
  'O Child, thy dignity
behold, in frankincense foreshown,
  take thou this gift from me.'
Our Lady covered with her gown
  her eyes from perjury.

'I wot that when with offering
  thou seest thy Father's face,
'Tis I that shall the censer swing
  in that most holy place.'

The third stood forth and bowed his head.
  'I bring a gift of myrrh.'
Our Lady crossed herself for dread
  when he looked down on her.
'I bring a gift, O Child,' he said,
  'meet for thy sepulchre.

'I wot that when thy lips are dumb
  and men defile thy head,
'tis I shall wait thee till thou come
  to be among the dead.

'When thou art neither king nor priest,
  thou shalt be friend to me,
when thou of all slain men art least,
  'tis I shall neighbour thee.

'But when thou sway'st thy golden rod
  or drinkest the new wine,
or goest in before thy God,
  with minstrelsy divine,

L

"tis I of whom within thy breast
  the hidden pledge shall be,
the prayer wherewith thou art possessed
  shall be a prayer for me.'

The Child upon Our Lady's lap
  the kings bowed down before:
to see this wonder, by good hap,
  the slaves thronged at the door.

Three kings rode out from Bethelehem
  to eastward hastily.
Our Lady caught, to save from them,
  the Child upon her knee.

LOVE

Then was the time when I on pilgrimage
  must go, and pass the whole round world about:
behold, your hearts were taken for my stage,
  and thereon now I call my chosen out:

twelve masters, twelve foundation stones of man
  at his creation builded into place,
twelve apostolic chieftains of his clan
  judging his world, twelve principles of grace:

of whom to-day I show you but these four—
  Peter who testifies how once I shone,
James who still feeds the fatherless and poor,
  And young Desire of Love, whose name is John:

Also Desire who hungers for quick gain,
  the necessary grudge that in you dwells
against my patience, your chief thorn of pain,
  Judas, the gate that opens on the hells.

THE RITE OF THE PASSION
For think not but hell hath its part in all
   that follow me, at my high feast to sit;
hear the world's captains utter now their call,
   ere each be yet changed to his opposite.

PETER

I, Peter, hastened to follow: in great awe
I also thy Transfiguration saw,
it was I who cried to thee: *Thou art the Lord*,
and I who struck to save thee with the sword.

JAMES

I, James, came forth to follow; yea, being called,
I, Boanerges, by thy might was thralled:
who would have smitten a thankless town with fire,
but find my anger changed to thy desire.

JOHN

I, John, have seen thee and have darkly known,
being also called and numbered with thine own;
with a voice of thunder have I cried for thee,
but O what dove's wings enter now in me!

LOVE

Yet have I one is mightier than all these,
who are her children and capacities;
they are friends and followers and apostles—she
is the soul that is chosen to be the mother of me.

MARY

O Son, long since in Cana at thy feast
did I not turn to thee when the wine had ceased?
but now I look on the whole world and see
there is no wine anywhere nor any glee,

L 2

but an end to feasting and an end to mirth
and cruel habitations through the earth,
and the mind unhappy and the soul undone;
therefore now I cry again to thee, O Son,
for entreaty, for a summons and a sign,
O Love, O blessed Love, they have no wine!

LOVE

Shall I not answer as then I answered thee—
O lady, what is that to thee and me?
We being perfected in our delight,
thou found in me and I in thee aright,
O elect soul, must we our joy unbind
to seek the dread salvation of mankind?
O miracle of grace, consider still,
know'st thou what doom this summons must fulfil?

MARY

They have no wine.

LOVE

Wilt thou have me pour out
that wine which is I to ease them in their drought?
All that is mine, O mother, is also thine:
what wilt thou have me do?

MARY

They have no wine. (2)

PART II

THE HERALD

We have seen Love in his years of ministry; yea,
we have seen him walking upon the world's highway,
   publicly vassal to folk of every sort,
a scavenger and a scribe, a prince and a priest,
nor ever his care hath stayed or his labour ceased;
   but who hath believed our report?

In twilit lanes his godhead of glory went
veiling his youthful lovers, or where the consent
   of friendship made peace more peaceful, at Caesar's
     court
where the high fair lords his gracious epiphany knew,
he at once, he only, and all things obeyed thereto:
   but who hath believed our report?

In miracles often, in parables often, he reigned
serving, and nowise the lowest task disdained,
   but the moment was secret, the moment was all too
     short;
and who shall remember? who shall be wise to know
that the light shall pass but the presence shall never go?
   who hath believed our report?

Who? unto whom is the arm of the Lord revealed?
who, being once by the glory amazed and healed,
   believes a myth that the tales of the world distort?
He is despised and rejected: and whose face is hid?
He is afflicted: who hath not mocked him and chid?
   who hath believed our report?

Who will cry to him *Love!* who will cry to him *Love, our
     fair lord?*
now when he gives no beauty and no reward,
     when the hounds are on him, the horns are blowing
     · the mort,
when the young god's face is pallid with stress of pain,
and he cries on his godhead, and nothing makes answer
     again—
     who hath believed our report?

Wonderful—lo, his wonder is blown away;
Counsellor—who shall ask counsel of him to-day?
     The Everlasting Father—his time is short;
the Mighty God—and his strength is less than a breath;
the Prince of Peace—but peace is come to its death;
     who hath believed our report?

Who will confess him now when the great sun dies?
who will confess him now in a darkness of sighs?
     who will confess him—after a foolish sort,
saying: *Thine only, thine, will I choose to be*—
who will confess him? who will betray him and flee?
     who hath believed our report?

LOVE

Lo I who once did your young beauty bless
now go upon my Father's business
into your clamorous market-place of sin.

PETER

Lord, thou art come now to its entering-in;
hear'st thou not how it shouts to welcome thee?

LOVE

All lovers have desired to look on me:
whose very nerves and sinews shake when I,
riding upon an ass, do first draw nigh.

JOHN

Lord, in thy kingdom seat us at thy side!

LOVE

Yea, can ye undergo what shall betide?

JOHN

Thy cup and thy baptism!

LOVE

No reward
give I though ye shall call me friend and lord.
I am the sole-begotten of Destiny,
and am your friend,—

JOHN

Only, O lord Love, be
still with us!

LOVE

Even now to the priests and scribes,
the rich men and the fierce barbarian tribes,
am I betrayed! and, led through my own band,
the feet of those who buy me are at hand!

JOHN

Lord, who is he hath sold thee to their wish?

LOVE

Behold, his hand with yours is in the dish
of daily food, his blood with yours hath run,
and what your weakness thought, his strength hath done.
Ye shall not move to save what he shall break,
he shall betray and all you shall forsake.

PETER

Though all forsake thee I will never fly!

LOVE

Before the cock crow on the day I die,
thou, my strong stone, shalt also fall on me
and I be broken, but even then on thee
will I too fall and splinter utterly
into fine powder, till the day shall come
when I shall build thee up to Christendom.

SATAN [to JUDAS]

Chosen of all Love's fellowship to sit
at the receipt of custom, being fit
to rule the exchanges of the flesh with God,
of the companions who with Love have trod
art thou the world's twelfth, keeper of the purse
and precious golden good Love doth disburse
with spendthrift zeal to gain some far delight
long promised thee but never brought to sight,—
good which this present moment might have graced:
O Judas, to what purpose is this waste?

JUDAS

Meseems a great necessity is near,
and many virtues whisper in my ear.

Intelligence bids break an outworn vow,
Desire saith 'Buy', and Prudence saith 'Buy now,
with Love's own person buy this present good'.
And ere these others too have understood,
to the world will I hasten, even I,
silver to gain, while they their foe shall buy,
such a great wealth is wholly mine to spend.

LOVE [to JUDAS]

That which thou hast to do, do quickly, friend!
Ere I shall wound thy head wound thou my heel.

[To the others]

But ye, who never sat at any meal
but as a Passover and memory
of your long exodus from the world to me,
I gather myself, I give myself, I grow
into the harvest of the seed ye sow:
I will be bread, and more than bread; and wine
and more than wine. I cry, *Come, come and dine*
on Me in yours: be new-emparadised,
take in your daily food your daily Christ.

SATAN

Also these have I overcome, not he,
Judas, alone, but even those great three
who were Love's chiefest heads of testimony:
Herod, who is Desire turned all to lust
of wealth, mad, miserable, and unjust,—
How art thou fallen, O John, O thou Desire!—
And Caiaphas the priest whom Sinai's fire
consumes no more, but Custom, that great cry,
barks in his voice at all steps equally.—

How art thou fallen, O Peter, O strong word!—
And Pilate, who is Service no more stirred
with passion, chill and weary government
by kings grown hopelessly benevolent.—
How art thou fallen, O James, when Love is naught!
These princes of destruction have I taught
to make Love void for ever, till his head
by time and earth and death is coverèd,
Love's servants to Love's self proving untrue.

JUDAS
What shall I have if I yield him unto you?

HEROD
Ten silver pieces,—and thy lusts withal.

CAIAPHAS
Ten,—and deaf ears for any new love's call.

PILATE
Ten,—and a rest from the journey that wearieth.

JUDAS
Follow.

LOVE
Ah, ah, I am weary unto death.
Tarry ye here while I shall go and pray;
O if this hour, my God, might pass away!

JOHN
Judas is gone, and in our souls' dark night
slumber hath seized upon me; fails my sight.

HEROD
Out of the lustful heart hath come forth might.

PETER

The word is lost he gave his folk to keep,
and we his church are fallen upon sleep.

CAIAPHAS

The gates are down; close and more close we creep.

JAMES

With eyes by utter weariness defiled
drowsily goes my care for wife and child.

PILATE

Now fades the dream whereby man was beguiled.

MARY

O Peter, keep good watch!—He sleeps. O John!
O James!—They sleep, and hark what feet come on!
O you his servants! wake; wake! Ah, 'tis you
in evil shapes, with blackening hearts, rush through—
the sword, the sword, the last sword pierces me!

LOVE

O lady, what is that to thee and me?

JUDAS

Whomever I shall kiss, that same is he.

LOVE

Could ye not watch? Friend, wherefore art thou come?

SATAN

Friend, he is mine and thine, the very sum
of all the world's betrayal: in this hour
God upon God hath loosed all Godhead's power.

One of the MINSTRELS

Three are the thrones that stand
   in the mid place of the world,
the trumpets by them sound
   and the banners are unfurled.
Three masters judge mankind
   where the peoples come and go—
religion, and government,
   and the wonder of a show.

High is the throne of the priest
   and the titles writ thereon;
wise is the learning there
   that the toiling soul may con;
God spoke in Sinai—
   this also Caiaphas saith;
wherefore the crowd draw near
   because he gives them faith.

High is Pilatus' throne
   with the lictors round about,
to guard the city ways
   where the folk go in and out;
peace upon earth he gives,
   commerce, and all increase,
and the people praise his name
   for that he gives them peace.

High is the throne of the king,
   king Herod that seeks delight,
with conjurers, dancing-girls,
   cupbearers, and men of might:

wherefore the people praise
his glory and come to see
all that the king can do,
because he gives them glee.

Love is come up for trial
before the thrones of the world;
where the ancient trumpets sound
and the banners dance unfurled.
Hear what those governors say—
hear how he answers them,
in the depth of your hearts to-day
as once in Jerusalem.

CAIAPHAS

Thou, Love, that hast made thyself of a worth unpriced,
make answer and say—Art thou the very Christ?

LOVE

Yea, also thou shalt see the Son of Man
coming with clouds of glory; in his van
wonder, behind him fierceness of delight—
I am I and Love is God; thou hast said right.

CAIAPHAS

What need we any further testimony,
for ye yourselves have heard his blasphemy!
He hath made himself God above all man's company
of dreams and visions—wherefore he ought to die.
Religion will not have him—bear him away
to Pilate that he may die this very day.

PILATE

Art thou the King of the Jews?

LOVE

Thou sayest it.

PILATE

Knowest thou not what judges here against thee sit?
Nor what they tell against thee, witnessing
thou hast published thyself abroad for God and King?
What art thou?

LOVE

Nay, if my kingdom were from hence
should not my servants fight in my defence?
But neither it is of this world nor they.

PILATE

Art thou a king then?

LOVE

Even as I hear thee say.
Therefore I came into this world to bear
great witness unto great truth everywhere,
and greatly they that are of truth rejoice
knowing me, seeing me, hearing my voice.
I, Love, am truth's sole witness.

PILATE

What is truth?
and what is love but a little piteous ruth?
O Caiaphas, whence is this Love brought to me?

CAIAPHAS

Surely he comes from Herod's tetrarchy,
the place of the flesh and fleshly lust and pride.

PILATE

By the flesh therefore let this love be tried,
and crown him or despoil him at his whim.
Bear him to Herod, that he may question him.

HEROD

Art thou that prophet we have heard of then so long?
Art thou that god, cunning and swift and strong,
who is king of the earth and all the heavens above?
Show us some pleasant miracle now, lord Love!
[Silence]
Some wonder of beauty, some loveliness again
thrilling the sense of nerves and exquisite brain;
let us be drunk with a fiery marvel of lust
saving our limbs from weariness and disgust.
[Silence]
Thou prophet, thou Love, that I may set thee free
work thou to-day a new desire in me,
by a magical knowledge show me a golden thing
made apt to delight me in my banqueting.
[Silence]
Wilt thou not? nay then, Love may die for me;
bear him back, soldiers, to his death—but ye,
joyous companions, come, for the hall is lit
and the wine is poured that we may drink of it.

PILATE

Even now I find in him no fault at all;
but ye, O folk, shall bid what shall befall.
O people of all the world! O Time and Space!
O ye who looked on Love in any place,
it is said before me that Love ought to die.
Behold the man!

ALL

Crucify! crucify!

PILATE

Shall I not scourge him and then let him go?

CAIAPHAS

If thou release him thou art Caesar's foe.
Hath not this talkative fellow in each town
sought ever to turn the whole world upside down?

PILATE

I am innocent of his blood; take heed, O priest:
shall I not loose him to you at your feast?

CAIAPHAS

On us and on our children be his blood.
Our house and our tradition he withstood.
He hath blasphemed our God, and he shall die.

PILATE

Even take him now, ye men, and crucify!

MARY

O Son, in a dark hour we bid good-bye.
Seven times as deep as any former pain
I feel the withdrawn steel pierce me again!

LOVE

O lady, what is that to thee and me,
seeing long since we knew these things should be?
for other sheep I have, not of this fold:
them also must I bring, out of night's cold

and hell's. But thou, my other self, content
these children, grievous in abandonment.
Lest mortal love in his dark hour have none
to strengthen him, mother, behold thy son,
dwell with him, cherish him. O mortal brother,
take to thy house thy charge; behold thy mother.

CAIAPHAS

This was thy son who rode upon an ass
to prove himself the god he dreamed he was,
but now can bring no mighty work to pass!

PETER

I fought till all the rest forsook him; say
no word that can me to their wrath betray.
No good can come of serving him to-day.

PILATE

Mourn, soul of man, for never shall our kind
a fairer or a falser vision find
than him whom now anguish and death shall bind.

JAMES

Come, woman; though destruction hide his brow,
and Love be God no more, yet canst thou sew
and cook for who in poverty lie low.

HEROD

Is this then she who bore this man and bred,
pleased that her love shall see at last his head
crowned, and him laid to-night in a soft bed?

JUDAS

Whether he die or reign I must with fire
tormented be, whom with all these his choir,
woman, he long hath racked with vain desire.

M

JOHN

Hearest thou not what all these witness? Thou
art all of Love is left unto us now.
Yet in my heart there is a house for thee.

MARY

God, God, why hast thou thus forsaken me? (3)

PART III

THE HERALD

Draw near, O people, let us crown our lord.
　Wherewith? With jewelled circlet or with thorn;
　let him, by knees as in his praise or scorn
bent, be with honour or reproach adored.
Let chain of gold or malefactor's cord
　bind round the mortal purple he hath worn:
　let him with outcry to his throne be borne;
for him be wine or vinegar outpoured.

God is he: hearken! this accusing tale
shall for his pain and ending best avail,
　in whose death-filmed eye breaks Deity.
Man is he: think not any thrusting spine
shall less be sharp for power supposed divine,
　or present darkness less for light to be.

Anguish of soul: bound in each bruised limb
　and manacled by tired feet, Love must go
　unto the Pavement, must with curse and blow
be pressed by the fear-ridden Sanhedrim.
Then from fierce hands and hate and faces grim
　shall he be barred by soldiery, that know
　naught but his name, with ordered spear-shafts. Lo,
hard on one side, the Devil, tempting him!

Anguish of body: bared to popular eyes
    and popular lips that mouth it and are fed;
last brute deforcement of the mysteries
    wherein the holy flesh is perfected,
the scourging at the pillar, and the flies
    that hum around the breast and bloody head.

O look no more for his descent. No more,
    while the crowd threatens and the priests despise,
    cry out upon him, but with mournful eyes
loosen his body. Lo now, he who bore
our sorrows, our infirmities, and wore
    our weakness as a garment, now Love dies.
    This man desires him and this man denies;
but who of all his people shall adore?

Call no more on him to descend; with myrrh
    anoint him, and remembering how he died
    keep yourselves yet for three days purified
with fasting: watch beside his sepulchre.
    We know not; surely Love may rise again,
    who on the cross of all men's hearts is slain.

SATAN

O Gabriel!

GABRIEL

O thou adversary!

SATAN

                            See,
can even the power of godhead slip from me?
Shall I not now destroy man utterly?
Look where the world comes out to see him die!

M 2

GABRIEL

Also yet more than this may they espy,
ere this hour ends, and thou perchance and I.

SATAN

Look where he stumbles already and falls down,
beneath the mockery of the roaring town,
striking again the head that wears the crown.

GABRIEL

See where the Cyrenean bears his cross;
and the women follow him in his hour of loss.

SATAN

See, where the sticks and spears about him toss!
as he goes up along the Dolorous Way,
and the Dolorous Strokes fall on him day by day.

GABRIEL

See, how Veronica wipes the sweat away.

SATAN

See, how they come now to the place of a skull,
where dry bones are the flowers that men may cull.

GABRIEL

The storm of voices empties in a lull.

SATAN

The sound of hammers is here the only sound:
why do the legions of angels wait around?
is there no help in any angel found?

GABRIEL

Veil, veil your eyes, O armies! height in height
from the youngest princeling seraph to the might
of Michael burning topmost, veil your sight!

be nothing at all about him any more
but an abandoned love; till all is o'er
do and say nothing, but adore, adore!

Neither how this is nor what this is ye know,
so far above you and so far below:
I only now to the last duty go.

I who did once before the Maiden move,
now to each heart that would itself approve
proclaim the tidings of the death of Love.

This is the moment when the world is riven
with the exalted mystery of heaven—
Nothing is given until all is given.

In his temptation and his agony
ye ministered beside him; now let be,
there is nothing at all to aid him now but he.

All ministration, all approach, is o'er,
question not, see not, move not; but outpour
in him your angelhood. Adore, adore.

For Love in his great hour must be alone.

SATAN

The work goes on; Gabriel, the work goes on.

GABRIEL

Do thou thy part then until all is known.

Father, forgive them, for they know not what they do.

SATAN

This is my part: from either end of time,
and from the coiled antipodes of space,
from the first life that issued from the slime
to the last life that falls away from grace,

I gather up the hosts of infamy,
   I loose the sevenfold mysteries of hell
that in the last encounter ye may see
   if love shall vanquish them or shall dispel.
I summon those who deal in chains and swords,
   affliction wilfully done upon love,
the torturers and evil-visaged lords
   who are most swift to make an end thereof.
Yea, come ye, all you people, to my side;
who is there by whose sin Love hath not died?

GABRIEL

From the last life that still can say *I am*
   being not yet made utterly one with Love,
to the least life that dare not wholly damn
   motions of Love that still within it move,
I call you; all his children, all his folk
   that have for Love's sake suffered any pain,
or known the ache beneath the dolorous stroke,
   come hither and see if that were but in vain;
come to the unfolding mysteries of heaven,
   the transmutations of the body of Christ,
the seven miracles of the Way, the seven
   witnessing words of Love self-sacrificed.
Yea, come ye, all you people, to my side;
who is there that for Love's sake hath not died?

LOVE

Who is there that will follow where I go?
   This is the first slow step upon the Way—
possess within you all that works you woe,
   put off all anger with it and all dismay.

O you at once the slayers yet the slain,
   you friends yet executioners of Love,
know by the anguish of your hearts' own pain
   how ye are guilty of the death thereof.
Come then with pardon, which is the bright speed
   I make to turn each foeman to a friend,
which is the mere refusal to give heed
   to aught but expectation of the End:
I cry aloud in God for them and you—
Forgive them, for they know not what they do.

      Woman, behold thy son.

SATAN

Look, look upon the world! where is the light
   that lately shone upon the streets and skies?
The common day returns, no longer bright
   with heavenly presence and divine surprise.
The common tenderness, the common care,
   can they, O dupes of Love, can they be he?
your earth's devices, that so many share,
   can they be lures to immortality?
O no, the royal dynasty and house
   whereto ye pledged your fealty now is lost;
be brave then, with your sight throw off your vows,
   and buy no fantasy at so great a cost!
This is not Love—that dream is quite undone—
this is but your mother, this is but your son,

GABRIEL

Who will be gentle, blithe, and debonair
   even when the miracle is wholly ceased?
who will make courtesy his daily care,
   whether he serve the greatest or the least?

who will attend his cousins with goodwill,
  even though his own heart faint for need thereof?
though duteous kindness be his only skill
  who late was vassal and blood-brother to Love?
Watch for Love's coming—but in others' need;
  ravage not the wide wilderness for a sign,
but in your nearest neighbourhood give heed
  to what least light may on those neighbours shine.
All else is Love's—this only must be given—
a gate, a place, an opening meet for heaven.

LOVE

Who is there that will follow where I go?
  This is the second step upon the Way—
to know I am born everywhere; to know
  the Child with the Mother doth not wholly stay.
There is no mother but is mother of me;
  Yea, though ye see not ye shall well believe
'tis I whereby at all ye do agree,
  and I whom in all loves ye must receive.
I have given the mystery of my coming-forth
  into the hands of lovers and of friends,
and happy he who there adores my worth:
  who adores me allwhere till creation ends.
I cry, while the world's cycles slowly run,
Son, lo thy mother! mother, lo thy son!

  To-day shalt thou be with me in Paradise.

SATAN

Ye who have stolen love by many a plea
  from others your companions; who have bound
the master of love and master of liberty,
  because in freedom only Love is found;

ye who have claimed love as your proper due,
  setting yourselves as governors over him;
ye who have busily begun to sue
  for love to ease an ache or please a whim—
ye who have brought him into bondage so,
  now when ye find yourselves on a like cross,
and, he unable to save you from your woe,
  clamour against his wounding and your loss,
in the good man's claim, the foul man's lechery,
cry out *Come down* in a common mockery.

GABRIEL

Who is there, O Love, that hath not done amiss,
  seeking to steal and seize and own the grace,
claiming of right some long-accustomed kiss,
  panting with greed of some new-visioned face,
but if they turn—see where they turn and run,
  my company and thine, dove-canopied Lord—
forget the thefts of Love they all have done,
  remember how they acknowledge their reward.
They stammer on the word *Thy will, not mine;*
  entreating still, with folly for a prayer,
that in thy kingdom thou wilt make them thine,
  yet cast not thou thy penitents to despair.
Robbers no more, they sigh *Remember me;*
show them thy favourable liberty.

LOVE

Ere I descend, ere I put off the last
  holy and sacred knowledge of my power,
ere all my godhead be quite overcast
  and I be fallen to my most bitter hour,

I cry in a vision, to all my folk I cry,
    all those I have loved and sojourned with so long,
you publicans and pharisees, who deny
    and who betray, who seize and do me wrong,
who spurn and mock me—yea, if but one word
    be loosed across the abyss to me and say
Ah Lord, remember me; in thy kingdom, Lord,
    in a vision I answer and cry to him *To-day,*
To-day thou shalt be with me in Paradise;—
Ah now, what now, what terror before me lies?

    My God, my God, why hast Thou forsaken me?

SATAN

Now I the Cross am risen with all my power
    to rule the thing I bear; now, you strong thrones,
come and behold how I above him tower,
    and beauty lying beneath me stirs and moans,
come and behold the triumph won through me,
    and have no other fear than that he die
and dying rob you of the perfect glee
    to know that Love is no more God most high;
come, all you who have grudged and scorned and sneered
    and anyways denied or hated Him,
yea, also who have fled from him and feared,
    his soul is fainting and his eyes are dim.
O my people, who amongst you will stand up
and put to his lips the last and bitterest cup?

GABRIEL

This is the time when ye can move no more,
    for the Cross bears you, no more you the Cross;
ye cannot choose now, as ye chose before,

for all the world is mere defeat and loss.
Darkness is o'er you, and about you death,
   and in the darkness only dying Love,
whom ye hear moan but know not what he saith;
   nor can ye, if ye would, at all remove,
for ye are fixed in him as he in you.
Now even the angels of your pilgrimage
cry to you, saying: 'Shall He make all things new,
   this refuse thrown out from the world's bright stage,
this naked, useless, wounded, frenzied thing,
that cannot heal himself of his suffering?'

LOVE

What now am I who hang 'twixt heaven and earth,
   being made a spectacle and a mockery?
Now even my chosen find me of no worth;
   they that pass by shoot out their tongues at me.
What sorrow is there that is like to mine?
   What pain of lovers like Love's very pain?
Behold, in my hands and feet I bear the sign;
   now even I know that even I am vain.
All that was I is given into the grave,
   part seized by violence, part fled by stealth:
others I saved, myself I cannot save—
   where is my victory? where is my health?
where my salvation? where my deity?
My God, my God, why hast thou forsaken me? (4)
      [A long silence]
            I thirst.

SATAN

In the taste of all the wells of idleness
   and all the running rivers of industry,

36

shall there be found no waters that can bless
  the infernal mansions with felicity?
All the adventures of the body, all
  the explorations of the aching mind,
these have found out all drugs ephemeral
  and now there is none left for them to find.
Wide and more wide I wander, and behold
  magic on magic fails to give me peace.
No youthful pirate and no prophet old
  shows me a land wherein my thirst can cease.
All things are tried and all things are accurst:
in a rich land of rivers still I thirst.

GABRIEL

Look on this company, O cherished lord!
  since dawn sprang on their souls they waited here
expecting when perfection should be poured—
  nor have they fled for weariness or fear.
Of the world's potions would they never taste—
  nor ease with seeming Lethe their desire;
here to thy buttery have they made haste,
  and shall thy grace not hear what they require?
O 'tis but thou they wait for! 'tis but thou!
  parched in the fevers and the droughts of Love,
they burn, they anguish, but they keep their vow
  who dreamed at dawn of springtime and the Dove.
Thou only best, and all things else being worst,
except thou give them drink they can but thirst.

LOVE

Out of the vanquished woe I turn again:
  I know you separately, I know you all.
O people of my heart, I feel your pain

come in upon me; now no more a thrall
unto a death beyond the deaths ye know—
    infinity's loss being gathered up in me—
I take your deaths into me; I bestow
    my presence on your infelicity.
Drink, drink, for I am given; do but taste!
    why for the brackish will ye leave the sweet
waters which I to bring you have made haste?
    is not that swiftness marked on hands and feet?
Nay, lies one heart in desert places curst?
still, while he drinks not, still *I thirst, I thirst.*

It is finished.

SATAN

It is not yet concluded; O not yet!
    Forbear to come upon us, O thou End!
Though all our hopes till now were overset,
    it may be that some hope shall yet befriend.
It is not finished; there is much to do,
    there is more and more to win and store and hold;
all that we gained is vanished, but who—who—
    can be content while aught is uncontrolled?
Be swifter, O be stronger, you my peers,
    grasp, seize, and ravish: beauty is your prey.
We have scourged her and slain her through these many years
    and shall an end come, and that end to-day?
It is not finished; strike, and strike again—
it cannot be that all things are found vain.

GABRIEL

It is finished! O what messenger, O what light!
    O hear! O is it silence, is it sound?
Naught can be wrong where all things are most right,

and this but foretells what shall more abound.
Deaf, lame, or blind—lo, the renewal comes:
    and these things are but knowledgeable joy—
be deafened now by that delight which numbs
    almost its own capacity and employ.
Be lame, new heavens so fast about us move:
    be blinded by this glory of delight:
and still love's healing issues out of Love—
    and still we are but on the verge of sight.
All things are old and all things are made new:
Truth—O most perfect marvel—is found true.

LOVE

Now with a great voice I begin to cry:
    I am wholly now and utterly come to pass,
ended and perfect is my ministry—
    I am the reflecting and burning sea of glass
imaging that wherewith I must be one.
    Beyond creation that within me lies,
O Love, am I not also found thy Son?
    Creation knows me in how many a guise,
but we are nothing save our Unity,
    which though awhile I was not, yet I was,
and am again most wholly come to be,
    the burning and reflecting sea of glass
which nowise can be dimmed now nor diminished;
lo now I cry with a great voice *It is finished.*

Father, into Thy hands I commend my spirit.

SATAN

They fail, they fail, they are dropping through nothingness,
    they are altogether falling into naught!
O Love, that thou mayst all creation bless,

these too to thy last precipice have I brought.
They that have had Desire for god so long
  feel a Desire much greater than their own;
a stronger power than theirs engulfs the strong;
  all that they showed to others they now are shown.
All that have followed the fire and not the light
  are lost in darkness of a roaring fire,
wherefrom the smoke of their torment to the height
  of benediction does no less aspire.
Since only through such change they reach the End,
into thy hands their spirits I commend.

GABRIEL

There is nothing more to be or do but thou!
  I loose these souls to thee; be thou their soul;
they watched for thee a little moment—now
  take and transform them, O thou perfect Whole.
Even now what rapture in the last long sigh
  impels them into that profound abyss
which is thyself, O God, O Love most high!
  Thou hast made them at first for nothing else but this.
Look, how they fall into thee, and are gone,
  where separation is not any more,
for all in thee are mightily made one
  where thou dost all their proper selves restore.
Hark, how each sighs, finding the perfect end,
Into thy hands my spirit I commend.

LOVE

Even I that am God, even I that alone am heaven,
  will keep the word that is its only law—
Nothing is given until all is given;
  I will make my City whole and without flaw.

Being risen throughout my being I take thee last,
 O tender flesh that wast with me so long,
bear this withdrawal till the hour be past
 and in myself I make thee newly strong.
Except, O pleasant dust, thou undergo
 the operation and high art of death,
how in thy own degree canst thou too show
 what now through all but thee my wisdom saith?
My Earth, that thou mayst in the Unity end,
say: *To thy hands my spirit I commend.*

GABRIEL

Out of the abyss life flows to earth again—
but the suspended ritual waits the slain.
The victory yet is dark, the victor dumb.
Ye officers of his entombment, come;
ye who are left, forlorn and desolate,
approach; undo the fastenings of his fate,
lift him with gentleness into the new tomb—
none, none before have entered in the gloom,
nor have ye yet, despairing, understood
the chill of the body, the congealing blood.
With yet-pierced hearts accept him and remove;
'tis love that waits upon the death of Love.
But ye, angelic armies, from the night
burn with fine rapture through the depth and height,
and cry, in adoration still renewed,
while lightly his entire beatitude
begins to ravage and to empty hell,
Praise to the Name who doeth all things well. (5)

PART IV

THE HERALD

Lament, O world! Love dies and let him die;
  bring him with ritual to his sepulchre,
nor let, to be a deep perpetual sigh,
  Time new-embalm his memory with myrrh:
    [All the Persons] *Love dies and let him die—*
Order the great procession; let all come,
but let their longings and their mouths be dumb.

Inter him with consideration; he
  was once a prince of a most royal house.
Bear him not slovenly or treacherously
  as those would do who have forgot their vows—
    Love dies and let him die—
nor in some plague-pit as an outcast fling;
though he was cast out he was yet a king.

He was the master of all households; he
  went forth with many lovers day by day;
in many friendships was his deity
  exalted in sweet joyous interplay.
    Love dies and let him die—
He hath wholly passed from knowledge and from place,
leaving our poor lives vacant of all grace,

All the fair glances, all the changing eyes,
  all intermingled clasp of hand with hand,
all adoration, all superb surprise
  that did about the things of earth expand—
    Love dies and let him die—
all salutations that can ever be
of such import, of such repute, as he;

N

all conversation, all instruction, fades,
   they were but ghosts that glimmered at his side,
and if he pass into the place of shades
    how should they any longer here abide?
     Love dies and let him die—
all knowledge passes and all song must cease;
death makes a solitude and calls it peace.

The slow civility of cities now
   breaks up within itself, and is no more;
the most of all delight is but to know
    there is something we a little less abhor—
     Love dies, and let him die—
a little less abhor than all the rest;
we are but quietly weary at our best.

Weary is Pilate in the Judgement Hall,
   and weary is the thought of Caiaphas,
weary is Herod though he vainly call
    for some new revel to be brought to pass—
     Love dies and let him die—
and the poor folk of each Jerusalem
are grown too weary even to strive with them.

Beauty is perishing in a doleful plight;
   and, beauty vanished, what more can we say
than in the morning *Would that it were night!*
    and in the evening *Would that it were day!—*
     Love dies and let him die—
we cannot aid him, we cannot restore,
nor can we bid him rule us any more.

Beauty is dying because Love is dead,
and Love is dead! Love, our fair lord, hath died!
Vain were the bloody drops his anguish shed;
we have no governor and we have no guide—
Love dies and let him die—
all sweet conclusion is with him destroyed;
there is nothing now within us but the void.

He was a fiery and most powerful god
and is trampled underfoot as a spent torch!
how vainly to his portals have ye trod!
there is no temple now beyond the porch.
Love dies and let him die—
His tabernacles are forsaken: come,
children of men, be tearless and be dumb.

[A Funeral March]

FIRST MINSTREL

When the strong son of David
held all things in his reign,
spirits and kings and peoples,
he murmured *All is vain.*

When the divine Alexander
looked over Ganges afar,
he found the weariness mighty
in all his host of war.

When the great Julius carried
Rome on his single breath
they asked him what end was fitting
and he answered *Sudden death.*

N 2

When the wise Cicero brooded
   on the purple and the thorn
he said, *Though death be a good gift*
   it is better not to be born.

When the most tender Virgil
   smote on the subtle strings,
this was the music that issued:
   the tears in mortal things.

When the proud English poet
   numbered his hours of glee
he sighed a single knowledge—
   It is better not to be.

Yea, all our wisest utter
   to-day one prayer of pain—
The roads are filled with darkness;
   let us not live again.

For hope is dead within us
   and the hope of hope is sped;
who shall be strong to harrow hell
   unless one rose from the dead?

SECOND MINSTREL

In a place of shades unknown
under a shadowy throne
the shades of men are blown
   after a dying dream;
no gospel there is heard
nor spoken any word,
only the shades are stirred
   by things that only seem.

THE RITE OF THE PASSION

For there each shade beholds
a vaporous cloud that folds
the shadowy throne and moulds
   likeness of its own face;
each over all sees naught
but his own imaged thought
into possession brought
   and having sovereign place.

Natheless, each yet is blown
with sad, inaudible moan
far from that cloudy throne
   and that which seems thereon;
wherefore continually
a flame begins to be
'twixt that which seems to see
   and that which it doth con.

A pale flame wakes and moves
and 'twixt those shadows roves,
which their pained dream approves
   for a perpetual fire;
and still their weary wings
labouring through cloudy things
feel the desire that stings
   and cannot end desire.

From flame to cloud they go,
and cloud and flame are so
that those shades nothing know
   except their own sad will;

for all dreams that abound
of all rich sight and sound
nothing is ever found,
   and nothing ever still.

Wherefore continually
is a great mystery
of things that cannot be
   and visions ever fled;
and how at all should they
find any rest or stay
or dawn of a true day
   unless one rose from the dead?

THIRD MINSTREL

When our Lord came riding
   through the midst of them,
the children ran and shouted
   in Jerusalem,
throwing down their palm-leaves,
   throwing up their caps;
all the babies crowed to him
   from their mother's laps.

When our Lord came swiftly
   through the place of shades,
all the children thronged to him
   fresh from Herod's blades;
the sad dusk was full of them
   whom he did retrieve,
and first the smallest of them all
   from the lap of Eve.

THE RITE OF THE PASSION
Socrates and Caesar
  though he met with there,
though he went a thousand miles
  to the bottom of hell-stair,
yet he came again to them
  when, turning from their play,
all those little Jewish souls
  observed the Sabbath day.

But within the garden
  he slept in double ward;
armed still and silent
  watched the Roman guard;
watched the high prince Michael
  astonished and aware
of a new thing moving
  as dawn filled the air.

And within the chamber
  he slept in single ward;
all the rock was conscious
  of the heavenly guard.
From the air within the air
  a soft wind came,
and above the silent head
  burned the tongues of flame.

FOURTH MINSTREL

Who is this that cometh
  as a wind from the south?
who is this that moveth
  with a song in his mouth?

who is this that laugheth
   since naught goes amiss?
who is this that sigheth
   as for pure bliss?

who is this that bloweth
   and the vapours flee?
who is this that signeth
   and the sick are filled with glee?
who is this that watcheth
   lest a sparrow fall?
who is this that meeteth
   with his friends in his hall?

This is Love in loveliness,
   this is Love in light;
this is Love that singeth
   of a tender sight;
of an old man happy,
   or a young man gay,
or a single dragon-fly
   in its blest array;

of two lovers meeting,
   or of rising birds,
or of a high minstrelsy
   mingling notes and words,
or of all sweet knowledge,
   all sweet thought above:
who is this that cometh?
   children, this is Love.

FIFTH MINSTREL

What great Apostle,
    When the Christ rose,
met with him secretly
    in the garden close?
fast ran Saint Peter,
    fast ran Saint John,
when they heard the rumour,
    but our lord was gone.
Only in the morning
    he was earliest seen
by a weeping spirit,
    Mary Magdalene.

Oft in a glory
    to my heart he came,
only-begotten,
    with love for his name;
but what bitter passion
    on myself for tree
hath his bounty suffered!
    now deep in me,
silent, unmanifest,
    hiding his power,
during a time and times,
    waits he his hour.

High imaginations,
    wait, sad and still,
till a sudden rumour
    your desire fulfil.

But, O blessed Magdalene,
when the first dawn
shines across my spirit
from that garden lawn,
watch with me, speak with me,
blind me with tears,
when angels fall silent
and himself appears.

SATAN

There is a thing that man may never do,
a mountain that his feet may never tread;
the mightiest power is snapped: bear witness, you,
children of our Lord Love, that he is dead.

Dead in your hearts the Love that lit you lies;
ye know that he shall never rise again.
Though you shall watch for ever with sad eyes
your whole lives' grievous vigils are in vain.

Hear ye the word which is creation die,
the Tree of Life is withered all and hoar;
in that dark separation which is I
Love fails from Love and shall be God no more.

Through all of Being to the bounds thereof
I search if aught of it may yet remain.

LOVE

Amen.

SATAN

O Voice, who art thou?

LOVE

I am Love,
And from destruction I arise again.

[A triumphal March]

LOVE

Now is the world unto its centre come
  and lo I am in its centre: O my few,
my strong, my loved ones, be no longer dumb,
  cry, cry aloud: *Who is on my side, who?*

I am crowned and mitred, I am king and priest;
  I swear by myself I will make all things new,
I in dyed garments coming from the east;
  cry, cry aloud: *Who is on my side, who?*

Fiery and fragrant am I come again:
  of all the deaths and martyrdoms ye rue
there is no moment that at all is vain;
  cry, cry aloud: *Who is on my side, who?*

I am Love, I am Love; I am risen everywhere,
  I am Love in all the hearts that turn thereto;
I in all fairness am the only Fair;
  cry, cry aloud: *Who is on my side, who?*

Who hath kept the vigil, and I did not see?
  who hath suffered the agony, and I never knew?
I am come upon them all with victory;
  cry, cry aloud: *Who is on my side, who?*

Ye who have watched one hour, behold, it ends!
  and I who end it am called Faithful and True;
I have made you free for I have made you friends;
  cry, cry aloud: *Who is on my side, who?*

Also my foes shall find in me their end;
  Caiaphas shall be lit with my new fire,
Pilate shall have a god to be his friend,
  and Herod shall desire man's last desire.

Out of the broken hearts in desert and den
  I hear the cry that lifts to Christendom:
Lo, I come quickly—
         [All the Persons]
                Even so, amen,
  master and lord; even so, Lord Jesus, come.

CAIAPHAS

Wide were my eyes and yet I could not see;
  albeit I taught religion to all folk.
  I could not hear nor tell Love when he spoke.
O Love, fair Love, sweet Love, remember me.

PETER

Fearful of death and reckless cruelty,
  I, who confessed that Love was God most high,
  did with great oaths refuse him and deny;
O Love, fair Love, sweet Love, remember me.

PILATE

I feared the toppling of Rome's royalty,
  and many poor men breaking up my peace,
  wherefore I would not that Love should increase.
O Love, fair Love, sweet Love, remember me.

JAMES

I, who beheld when on the mountain he
  was glorified and did with prophets talk,
  fled lest I should on this last journey walk.
O Love, fair Love, sweet Love, remember me.

HEROD

I sought the furthest pleasures that might be
and would have miracles wrought in my sight;
wherefore I knew not Love nor his delight:
O Love, fair Love, sweet Love, remember me.

JOHN

I who received a charge beneath the Tree
have kept a shelter for the innocent heart,
making desire a holy thing apart;
O Love, fair Love, sweet Love, remember me.

JUDAS

I fell into a foolish treachery
exchanging Love for a quick worldly gain,
whereby he dwells in peace and I in pain;
O Love, fair Love, sweet Love, remember me.

MARY

O Child, I have waited long and watched for thee,
and all that ever can be said or done
beneath the sky, all that is lost or won—

LOVE

O lady, what is that to thee and me?
Even but a ceremony and a sign
that what thy will asked mine hath brought to be:
didst not thou cry to me: They have no wine?

I have given them wine for ever: yea, in me
all these are known and I in them am known—
I am the Sole-Begotten of Destiny,
I am the way; I, Love, am God alone.

I am the close of all men's mortal dying,
   I am living in them as I for them was dead,
I am the defiling and the purifying,
   I am the union, riven or perfected.

There is none on earth that can have place beside me
   nor any of all the angels that is God;
there is none can know what mysteries betide me
   who am those mysteries and their period.

I am the Passion and the Crucifixion;
   I am the Silence and the Rising again;
both far extremes of joy and dereliction
   I draw to myself, and they make answer again.

Say, what art thou, my angel Satan?

SATAN

                                        Lord,
   I am thy shadow, only known as hell
where any linger from thy sweet accord.

LOVE

Say, what art thou, my angel Gabriel?

GABRIEL

Lord, I am nothing but thy annunciation;
   thy message and thy summons, and thy call,
the Gospel to all men of thy great salvation.

LOVE

And I alone am utterly all in all. (6)

THE LAST SALUTATION

Let there be set no name to this but one
written by God's finger evermore upon
a white, a shining, an immaculate stone;

yea, if there be amongst you here one power
who hath drunk the dregs of a most bitter hour
and found the oil grown dry, the wine grown sour;

and hath not failed, nor washed from off its brow
the bloody sigil of its grievous vow,
and hath said still: *Yea, also this is Thou:*

praise be to Love for the most happy grace
that still hath kept it in its steadfast place,
praise for the dolour and glory of its face:

praise for the ever-old and ever-new
beauty that shines thereover and therethrough;
and bring us also, O Jesus Christ, thereto. (7)

---

1. Holy, Holy, Holy; Lord God Almighty
2. The Heavenly Word, proceeding forth
3. At the cross her station keeping
4. Throned upon the awful Tree
5. Praise to the Holiest in the height
6. Hail to the Lord's Anointed
7. Praise, my soul, the King of Heaven

TALIESSIN'S SONG OF THE SETTING OF GALAHAD IN THE KING'S BED

THROUGH the palace the torches go;
  who follows there?
Camelot, Caerleon, London, Dover, Verulam,
  and Winchester.
All the cities of Logres come;
all the cities of Christendom.
Up the stairway the torches go;
  who there is gone?
Camelot, Lutetia, Ravenna, Alexandria,
  Byzantion;
even New Rome, even the sacred Crown,
even the immortal central town.
To the chamber the torches go;
  who goes with them?
Camelot, Eleusis, Mona, Hieropolis,
  Hierusalem.
All the priesthoods in order come,
and the priesthood of Christendom.
Into the chamber the kings-at-arms
  royally pour;
Camelot Engated, Dragon Seat, Excalibur,
  heralds before.
All the bishops and princes see
the end of priesthood and royalty.
Round the chamber the knights-at-arms
  stand, a strong line;
Camelot embattled, the noble princes sevenscore,
  the great king's design.
They who now, their armour shed,
bear the prince to King Arthur's bed.

o

TALIESSIN'S SONG OF THE SETTING OF

Into the chamber the great king comes
   and the great queen;
Galahad, in strength more than mighty towns of
   Christendom,
   paces between:
lovely, lovely in his power
as the king's throne, as the queen's bower.

Into the chamber the high prince comes;
   who on him tends,
Galahad, Rose of Gold, Fire of Lilies, Galahad?
   Singers his friends,
Taliessin and Percivale,
undo the buckling of his mail.

In the chamber the high prince turns,
   louting full low;
Galahad King Arthur's hand kisses and Queen Guinevere's,
   Lancelot's also.
To the lords and champions he
bows himself for courtesy.

Over the chamber a silence falls,
   for our lord prays;
Galahad, shining bud of victory, Prince Galahad,
   the Youngest of Days;
time now back from time is come;
to peace the Peace of Christendom.

To the high bed Sir Lancelot's hand
   aids him ascend,
Galahad, Helayne's delight, lilied son of Lancelot;
   King Arthur's friend;
gaze ye all, ye can but see
mystery, mystery.

GALAHAD IN THE KING'S BED

Galahad lies in King Arthur's bed;
   torches depart;
Camelot, Caerleon, London, Dover, Verulam
   have here their heart.
Darkness on the chamber falls,
and the watchmen keep the walls.

From their stations the watchmen call,
   as the night goes,
call through darkness *Galahad*, counter-call *Prince*
   Galahad:
   deep in repose
sleeps, the Mercy through him shed,
the high prince in King Arthur's bed.

EPILOGUE IN SOMERSET: A SONG OF THE MYTHS

[For ANNE, DIANA, JEAN, and MARY: made at their request]

ABOVE the rippling rivers, amid the swelling combes,
in gardens fair and flowered, in low and lovely rooms,
among the farms of Somerset, the sheep herds and the
smiths,
we walked by sun and starlight, and looked upon the
myths.

As in a place of mystery, Love's Hierusalem,
the holy sites are gathered, and watchful over them
a Mount of sacred olives looks out on sacred rooms,
so a wonder of great courtesy stood up among the
combes.

Within an English garden, below a beechen height,
the lilies grow in summer, and the souls that are as white,
the souls that are as lilies; and where barbarous people
strove
we walked with sudden laughter, and made music out of
love.

Beneath a common patronage, within a common grace,
we heard the supernatural sounds breathed far through
time and place;
in a secluded summer we saw the flaming crowns
of all the antique legends come riding o'er the downs.

Among the spears and scimitars, between the peacock
fans,
we saw the Orient glory whose name is Suleiman's,
and by the Great King's bridle the Sheban wisdom
glowed,
outside an English window, upon an English road.

EPILOGUE IN SOMERSET

Beside an English gateway, within an English porch,
the words of great antiquity arose as lamp or torch,
the aureoles of the casual names that yet can sound so high
their subtle invocation brings the gods of vision nigh.

A voice went calling by me, and ere the voice had died
I saw among the swelling combes Diana all enskied,
Diana of the Romans, Diana of the night,
the buskined maids about her, the hunting javelins bright.

A voice went calling by me, and ere the voice had ceased
the mother of the mother of God ascended from the east;
I saw the vigil ended, and the light of Israel come
where Saint Anne stood up to prophesy the tale of
    Christendom.

A voice went calling by me, and ere the voice was done
rose up our lady Mary, deep vestured with the sun,
a vision of two thousand years, a tower of mighty crowns,
one foot among the ships at sea and one among the towns.

A voice went calling by me, and ere the voice had stayed
came streaming o'er the wooded hills the banners of the
    Maid,
Jeanne and her company of peers within the fiery dark,
the myth of mortal valour that went heavenward from
    Arc.

I heard my own voice calling, and lo above the springs
the princess Michal walked in peace, between the striving
    kings;
calling a name of childhood—the gate of heaven's own
    hall
in the prince Michael opened, a flame angelical.

EPILOGUE IN SOMERSET

O fast and thick about us the dreadful myths went by;
they thronged the combes of Somerset, they thronged the
  English sky,
the legends of antiquity, the everlasting forms
who are lamps amid the darkness and torches in the
  storms.

And by those mortal courtesies invited and ensouled
I saw my Mantuan Duchess, a darkness turned to gold,
where unadorned among them she lifted up her head,
touched by the work alchemical, in union perfected.

In unconcluded verse I named the heavenly Mount of
  Rome,
the hill of Saint John Lateran, whence shining thoughts
  have come
on Augustinian errand all the Saxon thanes must con;
I named the names of splendour—elect Byzantion;

the queen Iseult of Cornwall, with Tristram at command;
the queen Morgause of Orkney, with Lamoracke at hand;
King Arthur and Lord Lancelot, and crimson in his mail,
serving the last Achievement, the Master of the Grail.

O song amid the rivers! O laughter 'mid the combes!
O wonder in the gardens and beauty in the rooms!
O myth on myth arising, and cast among them thus
the crying of the sacred word the Sunday sang to us:

'He shall not let that Holy Thing which is abroad on
  earth
fail from the house of friendship, the place of joy and
  mirth;
by all the myths and legends, by the tale of Christendom,
He shall not let His Holy One into corruption come'.

EPILOGUE IN SOMERSET

The night is on the rivers; the night is on the combes;
a dozen lights are shining in far-divided rooms;
but deep within the firmament, high over sun and star,
where the great myths dwell for ever, the days of Aisholt
are.

AISHOLT,
by permission of GOD and OLIVE WILLIS,
August 1930

www.ingramcontent.com/pod-product-compliance
Lightning Source LLC
Chambersburg PA
CBHW021200090426
42740CB00008B/1167